Ten

abou_

ex libris

FOR MAY
DEC 2021

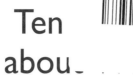

Candlestick Press

HAPPY
CHRISTMAS

SECRET
SANTA

Published by:

Candlestick Press,
Diversity House, 72 Nottingham Road, Arnold, Nottingham NG5 6LF
www.candlestickpress.co.uk

Design and typesetting by Craig Twigg

Printed by Ratcliff & Roper Print Group, Nottinghamshire, UK

Selection and Introduction © Jonathan Edwards, 2021

Cover illustration © Hugh Ribbans, 2021
www.hughribbans.com

Candlestick Press monogram © Barbara Shaw, 2008

© Candlestick Press, 2021

ISBN 978 1 907598 89 0

Acknowledgements

The poems in this pamphlet are reprinted from the following books, all by permission of the publishers listed unless stated otherwise. Every effort has been made to trace the copyright holders of the poems published in this book. The editor and publisher apologise if any material has been included without permission or without the appropriate acknowledgement, and would be glad to be told of anyone who has not been consulted.

Thanks are due to all the copyright holders cited below for their kind permission:

Liz Berry, *Black Country* (Chatto & Windus, 2014); Sujata Bhatt, *Collected Poems* (Carcanet Press, 2013); Gillian Clarke, *Selected Poems* (Carcanet Press, 2016); Jonathan Edwards, first published here, by kind permission of the author; Thomas Lux, *Selected Poems* (Bloodaxe Books, 2014) Houghton Mifflin, www.bloodaxebooks.com; Helen Mort, *No Map Could Show Them* (Chatto & Windus, 2016) by permission of Rogers, Coleridge and White; John Ormond, *Collected Poems*, ed. Rian Evans (Seren, 2013) by kind permission of the John Ormond Estate; Kathryn Simmonds, *Sunday at the Skin Launderette* (Seren 2008) by permission of Rogers, Coleridge and White; James Tate, *The Germ: A Journal of Poetic Research*, 2005 with kind permission of The Estate of James Tate.

All permissions cleared courtesy of Swift Permissions
swiftpermissions@gmail.com

Where poets are no longer living their dates are given.

Contents   **Page**

Introduction

What shall we do with work? Curse it, hate it, make escape plans from it, call in sick to it, write apologetic e-mails to it, still we find, every morning, we have to do it. What sort of fool would invent a thing like work? What sort of fool would do it? And what can the poets do to soothe or to heal us?

Work can inspire writers to great beauty. There are celebrations here of all sorts of workers, from folk who build cathedrals to those who drive taxis. In Liz Berry's great poem, a schoolteacher's average day involves conducting orchestras and experiments, guiding tiny hands through the safe use of scissors. Walt Whitman, in his gorgeously all-embracing way, seeks to celebrate and empathise with *all* workers, *everywhere.*

Compassion for experience that often goes ignored or unconsidered is a strength of poetry, and these poems allow us to share time and experience with a girl who fills her days gathering cow dung from the road, a mother working in the sex industry on Boxing Day.

Among the interesting things work does is the way it creates the routines of our days, schedules things, gives us experiences we wouldn't otherwise have. Thomas Lux's wonderful hymn to a commute is among poems that inspired my own celebration of my father's pedal-powered work journey in the 1950s.

Work can give us everything, from comedy to tragedy. James Tate's 'Brittle Family Photographs' never fails to make me laugh out loud. Coming from the South Wales Valleys, I've always been moved by poems of protest and dissent, the righteous anger of workers. I love Gillian Clarke's beautiful and emotive elegy to the victims of the Six Bells colliery disaster.

So, when it comes to the subject of work, it's amazing where poems take us. Mark Twain once wrote, "Work consists of whatever a body is obliged to do. Play consists of whatever a body is not obliged to do." Whatever else it is work does, how wonderful that it made these poems.

Jonathan Edwards

Cathedral Builders

They climbed on sketchy ladders towards God,
With winch and pulley hoisted hewn rock into heaven,
Inhabited sky with hammers, defied gravity,
Deified stone, took up God's house to meet Him,

And came down to their suppers and small beer;
Every night slept, lay with their smelly wives,
Quarrelled and cuffed the children, lied,
Spat, sang, were happy or unhappy,

And every day took to the ladders again;
Impeded the rights of way of another summer's
Swallows, grew greyer, shakier, became less inclined
To fix a neighbour's roof of a fine evening,

Saw naves sprout arches, clerestories soar,
Cursed the loud fancy glaziers for their luck,
Somehow escaped the plague, got rheumatism,
Decided it was time to give it up,

To leave the spire to others; stood in the crowd
Well back from the vestments at the consecration,
Envied the fat bishop his warm boots,
Cocked up a squint eye, and said, "I bloody did that".

John Ormond (1923 – 1990)

Taxi Drivers

They lean against the glossy buttocks of their cabs,
kicking free of clutch and brake,

stubble-headed, right arm browner than the left,
legs whitely shocking in their shorts,

their talk, impossible to tell when distance
seals their opinions off like glass.

Five cabs ahead, the leader takes a fare, shifts
into second gear, sweeps

out of the terminal and into startling sun.
Meanwhile they wait,

June sparkling on the river's filth a mile away,
the city folded tightly in their heads.

Kathryn Simmonds

Brittle Family Photographs

It's hard work and the pay is low, but at
least you get to hang out with a bunch of nasty,
bitter people. So I took the job. The first
week I thought I'd die. I couldn't stop my hands
from bleeding, and my legs could barely hold me
up. The second week my eyes were blurred and I
couldn't keep my food down. By the fourth week
I was beginning to like it. I felt strong. After
a year I felt nothing. I didn't know my name,
I didn't know where I was. Whatever it was I
was supposed to do got done, but I don't know how.
Then I met Deidre in the cafeteria and she said,
"Mr. President, you're doing a great job." "What
did you call me?" I said. "Mr. President," she
said. "How time pisses away," I said. "I can
hear the birdies singing." My eye was on the
Jell-O.

James Tate (1943 – 2015)

from A Song for Occupations

A song for occupations!
In the labor of engines and trades and the labor of fields I find the
    developments,
And find the eternal meanings.

Workmen and Workwomen!
Were all educations practical and ornamental well display'd out of
    me, what would it amount to?
Were I as the head teacher, charitable proprietor, wise statesman,
    what would it amount to?
Were I to you as the boss employing and paying you, would that
    satisfy you?

The learn'd, virtuous, benevolent, and the usual terms,
A man like me and never the usual terms.

Neither a servant nor a master I,
I take no sooner a large price than a small price, I will have my
    own whoever enjoys me,
I will be even with you and you shall be even with me.

If you stand at work in a shop I stand as nigh as the nighest in the
    same shop,
If you bestow gifts on your brother or dearest friend I demand as
    good as your brother or dearest friend,
If your lover, husband, wife, is welcome by day or night, I must be
    personally as welcome,
If you become degraded, criminal, ill, then I become so for your sake,
If you remember your foolish and outlaw'd deeds, do you
    think I cannot remember my own foolish and outlaw'd deeds?
If you carouse at the table I carouse at the opposite side of the table,
If you meet some stranger in the streets and love him or her, why
    I often meet strangers in the street and love them.

Why what have you thought of yourself?
Is it you then that thought yourself less?
Is it you that thought the President greater than you?
Or the rich better off than you? or the educated wiser than you?

(Because you are greasy or pimpled, or were once drunk, or a thief,
Or that you are diseas'd, or rheumatic, or a prostitute,
Or from frivolity or impotence, or that you are no scholar and never
saw your name in print,
Do you give in that you are any less immortal?)

Walt Whitman (1819 – 1892)

Muliebrity

I have thought so much about the girl
who gathered cow dung in a wide, round basket
along the main road passing by our house
and the Radhavallabh temple in Maninagar.
I have thought so much about the way she
moved her hands and her waist
and the smell of cow dung and road-dust and wet canna lilies,
the smell of monkey breath and freshly washed clothes
and the dust from crows' wings which smells different –
and again the smell of cow dung as the girl scoops
it up, all these smells surrounding me separately
and simultaneously – I have thought so much
but have been unwilling to use her for a metaphor,
for a nice image – but most of all unwilling
to forget her or to explain to anyone the greatness
and the power glistening through her cheekbones
each time she found a particularly promising
mound of dung –

Sujata Bhatt

Rachel in Attercliffe

I'm in suspenders, working Boxing Day.
Your dad, your boyfriend nips out for a beer
then indicates down Derek Dooley Way.
The sign outside says *entrance at rear*.
There's tinsel round the bannister, a star
above each bedroom door. I'm crimson to my hips.
I let them lift the layers and unhook my bra.
They're talkative, telling me what the kids
got yesterday. I smile. I don't mention my son.
Sometimes, I say I work in mental health.
The ones who're silent when they come
intrigue me most. You have to laugh at yourself.
I like to think there's hospital, a recently-dead wife.
I like to think I'm saving someone's life.

Helen Mort

What I See When I Drive to Work
(Boston to New York)

On clear days it's fast black dead west sixty miles
New England blazing or granite-brown
on both sides of the slide. Then a dip south-
west – the sun on my left cheek now flat
on my chest, and I'm warm,
with the other citizens, driving
to work. About lunchtime

I hit Hartford (each week a honk
for Wallace Stevens) – half a day done
for the insurance clerks and I'm halfway
to work. Twenty or so miles later,
on the arc of a long dropping curve, the sun
takes a quarry's gouged-out bowl.
I like the big machines, drills

and dozers, that eat
the rock and break it down to sand – at least
more than I like the insurance industry;
and then a town's announced
by a giant Jesus' coat rack
on a rubbled hill. It overlooks
a happy, placid burg known for brass

where I never stop
for gas or sandwich. I'm driving
to work – talk radio/gun control, Squantz
Pond, lunch pail, Ruby Road, never-cross-
a-picket-line, on my way
to earn a wage: Massachusetts, Connecticut,
and now nudging into New York,

just over which border
I follow for a few miles a river
that opens to a lake
that each day this fall
is open to more and more ducks,
which makes me happy, at this point,
driving to work with the rest of America,

who mostly get there before I do.
The last leg's most scenic, woodsy,
and takes me past a publishing complex,
Reader's Digest, Inc., massive buildings
on a hill, where a man someday
might reduce this poem to haiku.
I'm nearing now and exit by the exit

by the blind school – two more miles,
if I take the shortcut past some mansions,
to my office, which is
199.4 mi.
from my home. It's a lengthy motoring,
but the work is honest
and the customers human.

Thomas Lux (1946-2017)

My Father Cycling Up a Hill, 1957

It's the hill from the bottom of Factory Trip
all the way up to Manor Farm –
a *Welsh* hill, one long steep and steady climb

to nowhere, punctuated by the occasional sharp
or suicidal incline. These
are his feet, his calves – they're pushing,

pushing against the weight of the side
of beef or lamb in the basket
on the front of his bike. From his uncle's

butcher's shop to Manor Farm is a climb so far
if I were doing it now, by car, I'd think
twice. By bike? No way! Yet there

he is, my father, twelve years old, the weight
of the hill on his legs, setting out
once a week all winter, to deliver

the Sunday joint to Old Man Hodge. These
are his feet, the look on his face
as he pushes, pushes. This is the sweat

on his brow. His uncle pays him
in promises, end-of-week scraps, the back
of his hand. It's silly to know

what I do: my father is doing this
for his mother, his younger brother,
for his own father, who hasn't worked properly

since he got back from the war. This
is his front wheel, squeaking,
squeaking as he inches up that hill. I know

all the reasons he's doing this
and I wasn't even born then, so it's silly as can be
to know what I do – that he was doing it all –

look at him, pushing and pushing all afternoon – for me.

Jonathan Edwards

Miss Berry

I have learnt to write rows of o's bobbing
hopeful as hot air balloons from the line's tethers

and watched eight springs of frogspawn
grow legs but never...

and conducted clashy-bashy orchestras
of chime bars ocarina thundering tambour

and curled my hand over another hand
to hinge the crocodile jaws of the scissors.

I have accompanied a small mourning party
to a blackbird's burial plot

and rolled countless bodies, like coloured marbles,
across gym mats

and conducted science's great experiments
using darkened cupboards, plastic cups and cress

and unhooked a high window on a stuffy day
and heard the room's breath.

I have measured time by paper snowflakes,
blown eggs, bereft cocoons

and waved goodbye in summer so many times
that even in September my heart is June.

Liz Berry

Six Bells

for the forty-four miners killed in the explosion on 28 June 1960

Perhaps a woman hanging out the wash
paused, hearing something, a sudden hush,

a pulse inside the earth like a blow to the heart,
holding in her arms the wet weight

of her wedding sheets, his shirts. Perhaps
heads lifted from the work of scrubbing steps,

hands stilled from wringing rainbows onto slate,
while below the town, deep in the pit

a rock-fall struck a spark from steel, and fired
the void, punched through the mine a fist

of blazing firedamp. As they died,
perhaps a silence, before sirens cried,

before the people gathered in the street,
before she'd finished hanging out her sheets.

Gillian Clarke